SCRATCH & PLAY
MYSTERY WORD
PUZZLES

SHAWN KENNEDY

PUZZLE
WRIGHT
PRESS

An imprint of Sterling
Publishing Co., Inc.

www.puzzlewright.com

Puzzlewright Press and the distinctive Puzzlewright Press logo
are registered trademarks of Sterling Publishing Co., Inc.

2 4 6 8 10 9 7 5 3 1

Published by Sterling Publishing Co., Inc.
387 Park Avenue South, New York, NY 10016
© 2010 by Shawn Kennedy
Distributed in Canada by Sterling Publishing
C/o Canadian Manda Group, 165 Dufferin Street
Toronto, Ontario, Canada M6K 3H6
Distributed in the United Kingdom by GMC Distribution Services
Castle Place, 166 High Street, Lewes, East Sussex, England BN7 1XU
Distributed in Australia by Capricorn Link (Australia) Pty. Ltd.
P.O. Box 704, Windsor, NSW 2756, Australia

Printed in China

Sterling ISBN 978-1-4027-7458-4

For information about custom editions, special sales, premium and
corporate purchases, please contact Sterling Special Sales
Department at 800-805-5489 or specialsales@sterlingpublishing.com.

HOW TO PLAY

The object is to guess a 5-letter Mystery Word that contains no repeated letters.

To guess the word, scratch off letters in the Letter Grid. Scratch the first letter of your guess word in Column 1, the second letter of your guess word in Column 2, the third letter of your guess word in Column 3, the fourth letter of your guess word in Column 4, and the last letter in Column 5.

Beneath each letter is a symbol. An ✖ means that particular letter does not appear in the Mystery Word. An arrow of any kind means that particular letter appears in the Mystery Word but in a different position. A star indicates that particular letter appears in the Mystery Word in that exact position.

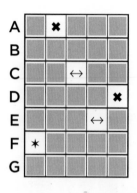

Use logic and information revealed from your guesses to deduce the Mystery Word.

For example, to guess the word FACED, you'd scratch the squares shown at right. The symbols revealed indicate that F is in the correct position (star), C and E are in the incorrect positions (arrows), and A and D do not appear in the Mystery Word (✖'s).

Given this information, you know that the Mystery Word must fit one of the patterns below.

F _ _ _ _
 E E   E
 C   C C

FE?C?   F?EC?
FE??C   F?E?C
FCE??   F??CE
FC??E

Since no common word has the pattern FC???, both FCE?? and FC??E can be eliminated. The C, then, has to appear in the fourth or fifth position.

Patterns FE??C and F?E?C can be eliminated since no common word has either pattern. Thus, the Mystery Word must fit the pattern F??C? and contain an E in either the second, third, or fifth position (FE?C?, F?EC?, or F??CE). For your next guess, you might try FETCH, FLECK, or FORCE but not FARCE, since your first guess told you that the letter A does not appear in the Mystery Word. FENCE isn't possible because it repeats a letter.

Continue in this fashion until you deduce the Mystery Word or use up all seven guesses.

As you become more skilled at the game, limit yourself to 6 guesses, then 5, and perhaps even 4 or 3.

All Mystery Words appear in the 11th Edition of Merriam-Webster's Collegiate Dictionary. No proper nouns are used except those that are also regular, uncapitalized words.

WORD #1

WORD #1

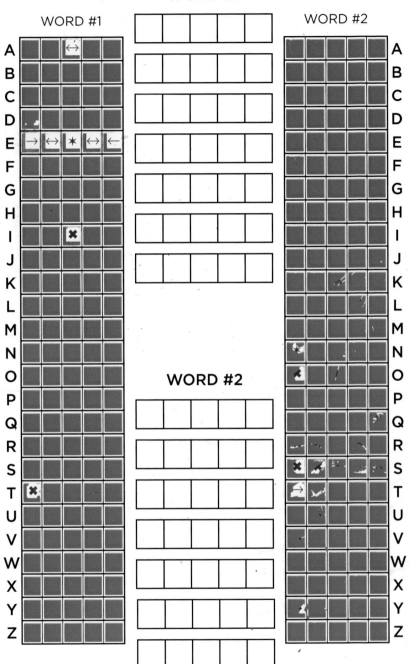

WORD #2

4

WORD #3

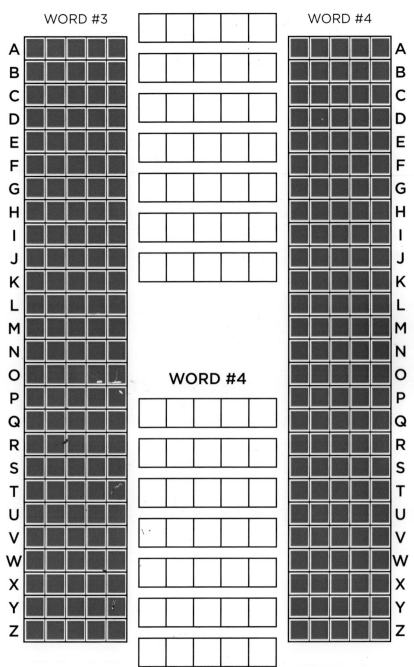

WORD #3

WORD #4

WORD #4

5

WORD #5

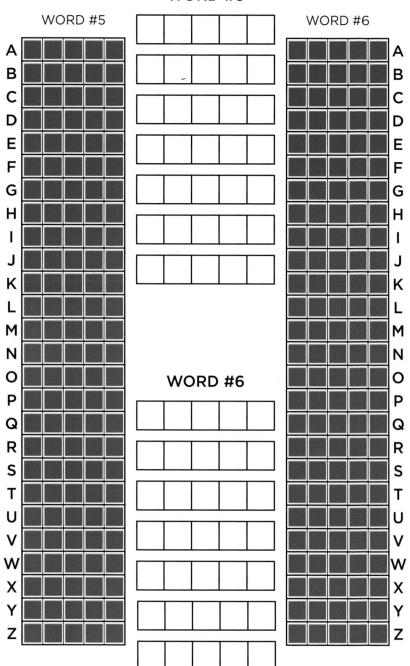

WORD #5

WORD #6

WORD #6

6

WORD #7

WORD #7

WORD #8

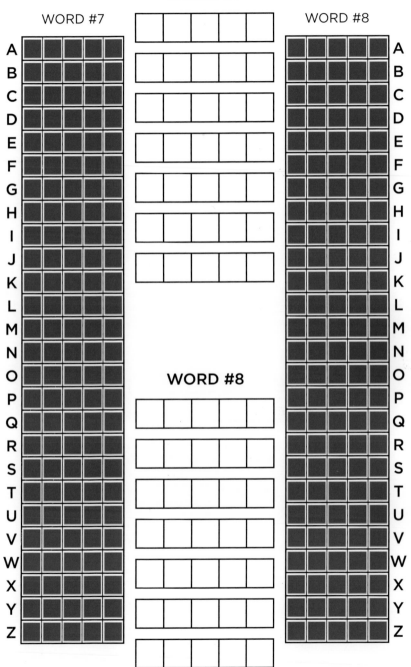

WORD #8

WORD #9

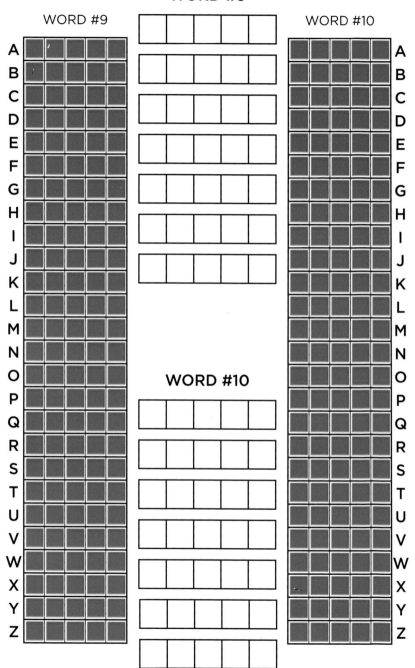

WORD #9

WORD #10

WORD #10

8

WORD #11

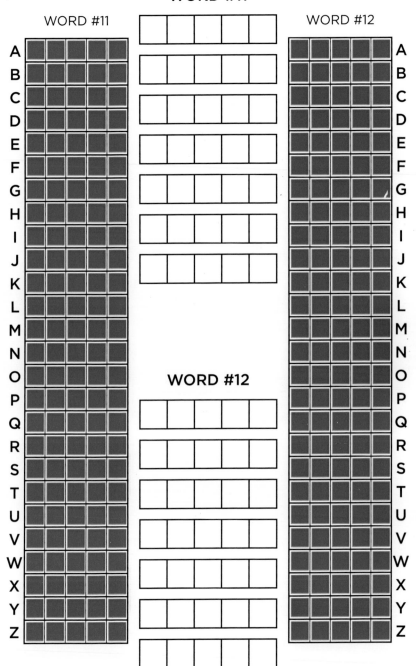

WORD #11

WORD #12

WORD #12

9

WORD #13

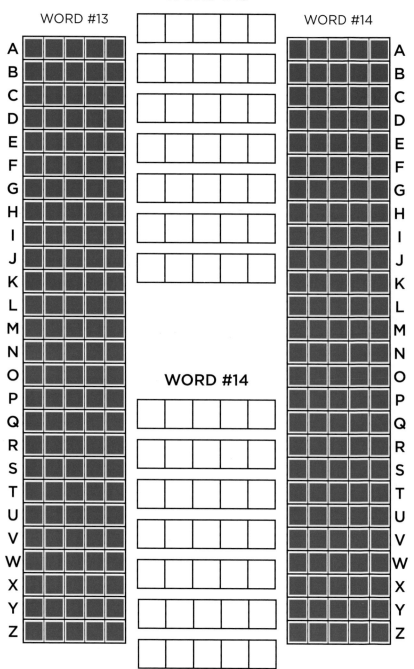

WORD #13

WORD #14

WORD #14

10

WORD #15

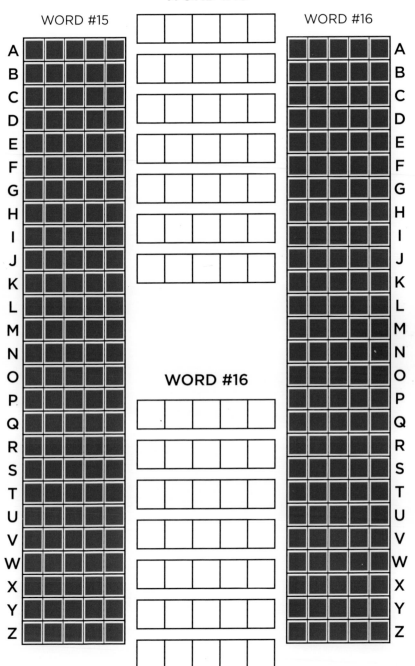

WORD #17

WORD #18

WORD #18

12

WORD #19

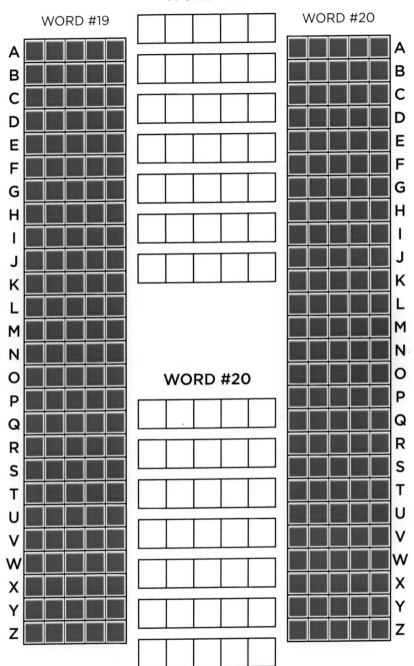

WORD #21

WORD #21

WORD #22

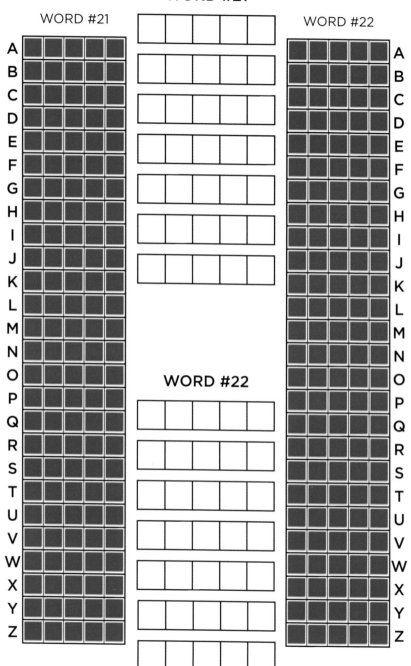

WORD #22

WORD #23

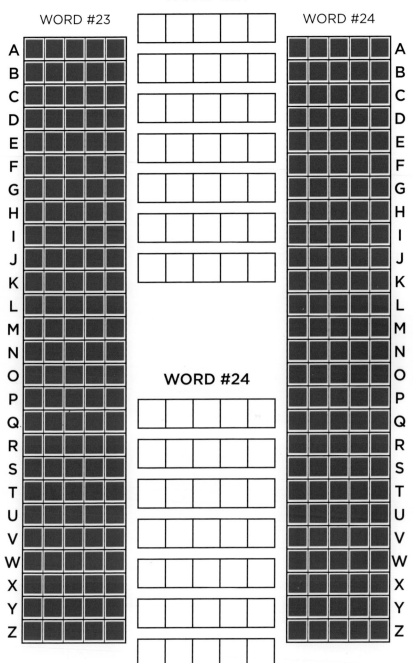

WORD #23

WORD #24

WORD #24

WORD #25

WORD #26

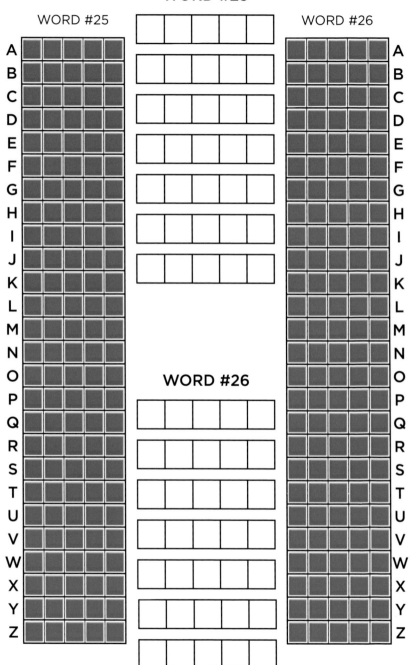

WORD #26

WORD #27

WORD #27

WORD #28

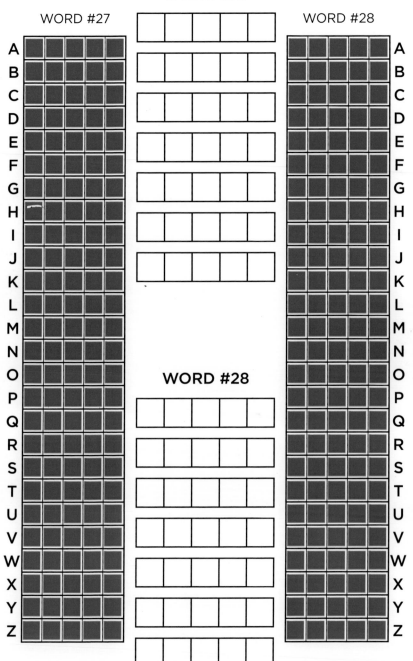

WORD #28

17

WORD #29

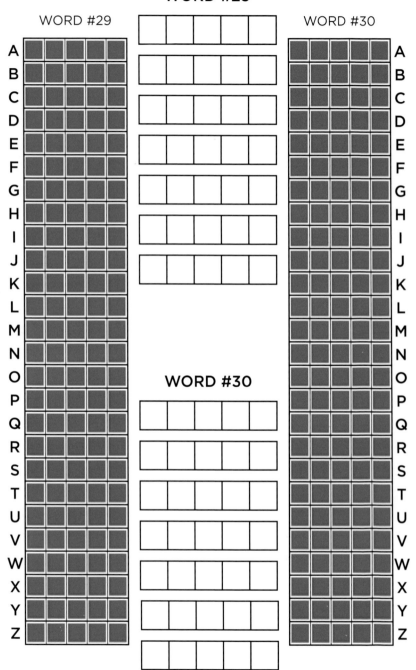

WORD #29

WORD #30

WORD #30

WORD #31

WORD #31

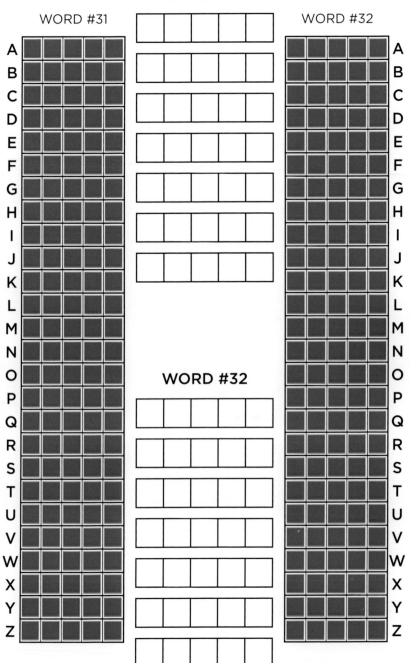

WORD #32

WORD #32

WORD #33

WORD #33

WORD #34

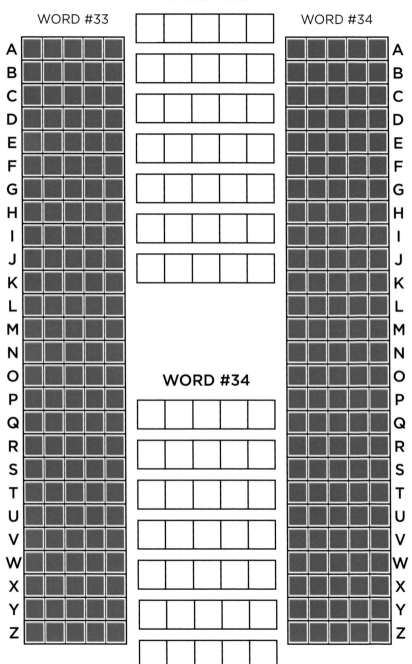

WORD #34

WORD #35

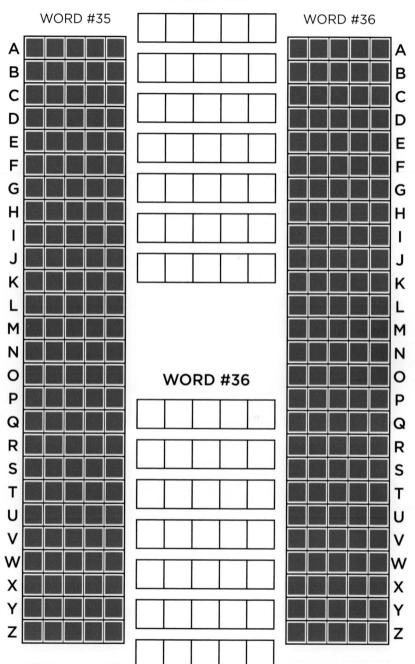

WORD #37

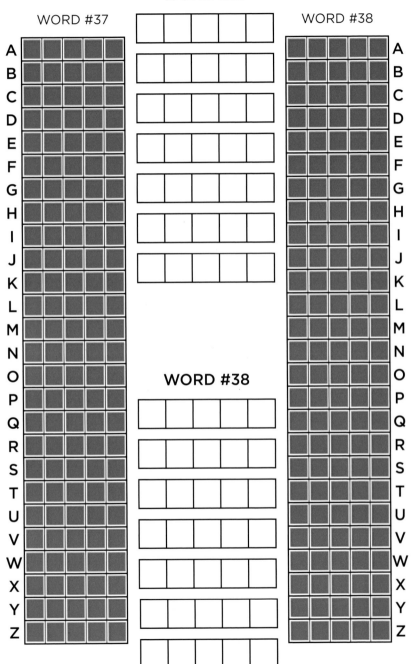

WORD #37

WORD #38

WORD #38

WORD #39

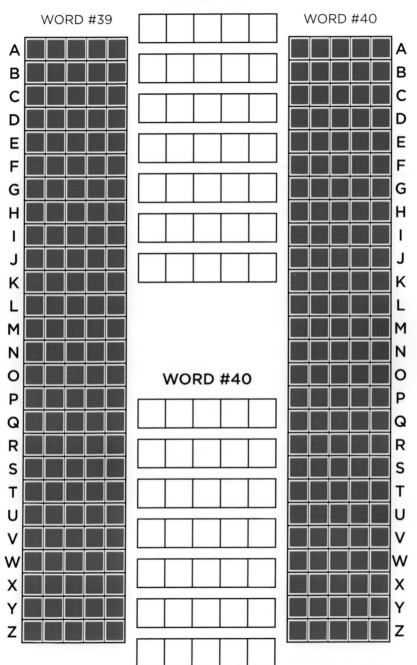

WORD #41

WORD #41

WORD #42

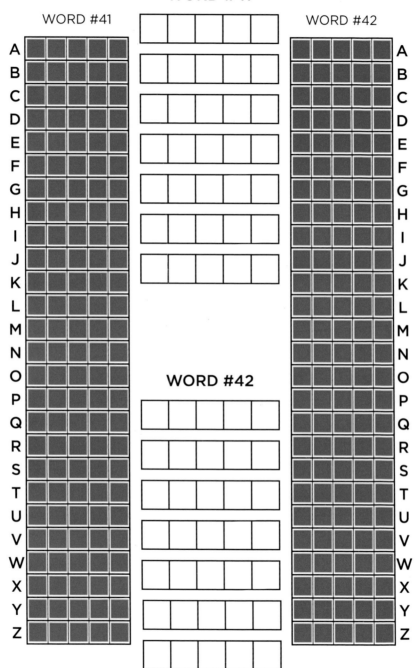

WORD #42

WORD #43

WORD #43

WORD #44

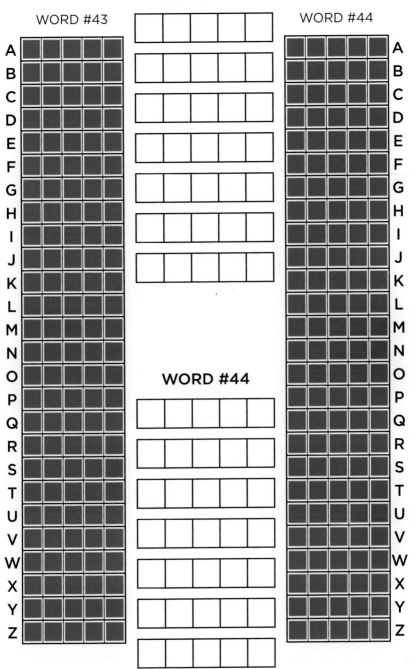

WORD #44

WORD #45

WORD #45

WORD #46

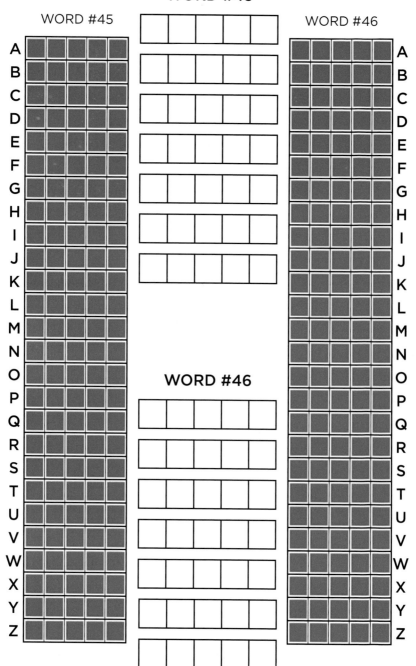

WORD #46

WORD #47

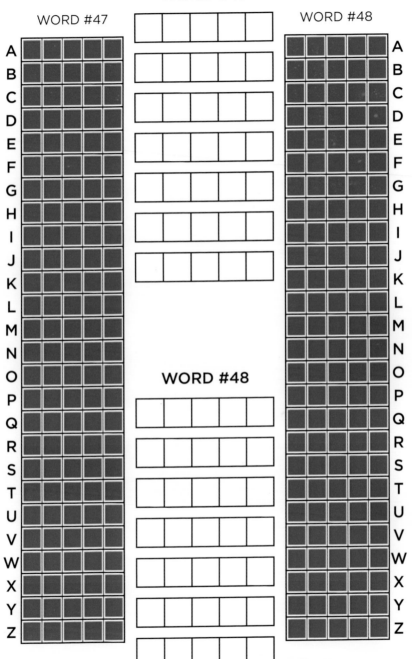

WORD #47

WORD #48

WORD #48

27

WORD #49

WORD #49

WORD #50

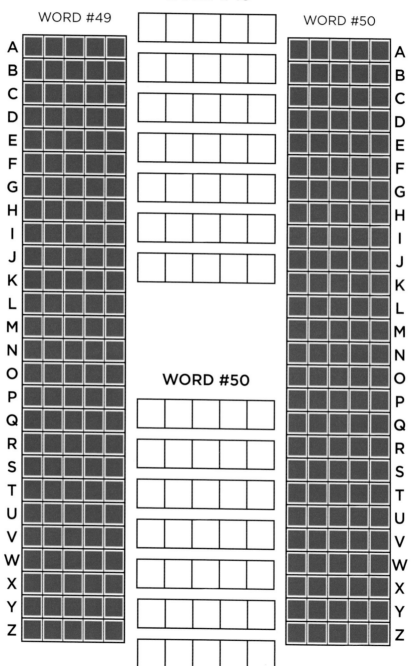

WORD #50

WORD #51

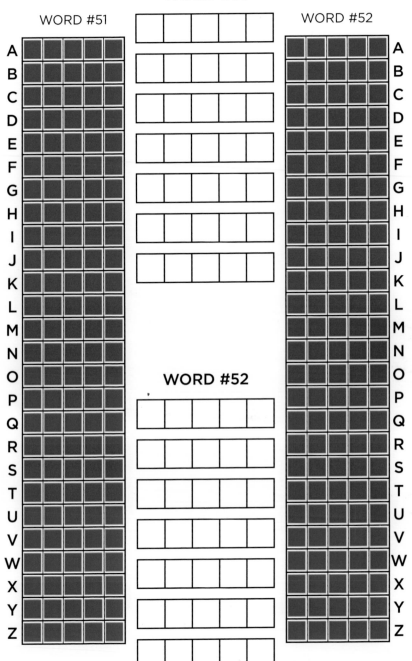

WORD #51

WORD #52

WORD #52

WORD #53

WORD #53

WORD #54

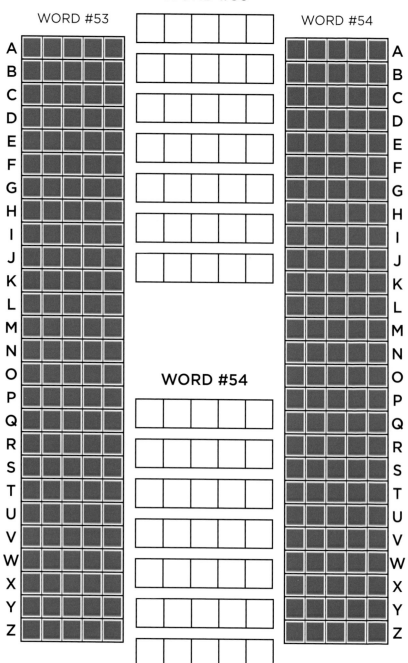

WORD #54

WORD #55

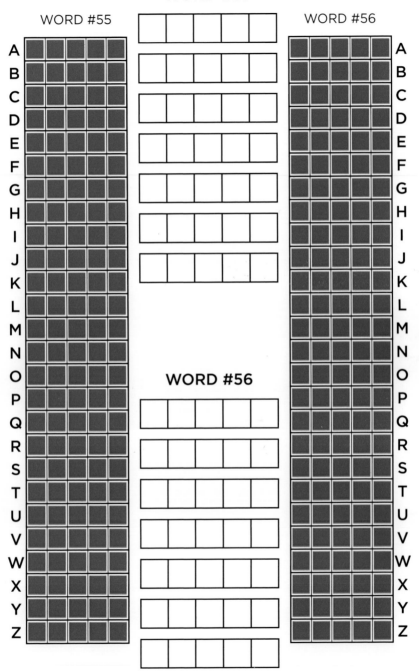

WORD #55

WORD #56

WORD #56

WORD #57

WORD #57

WORD #58

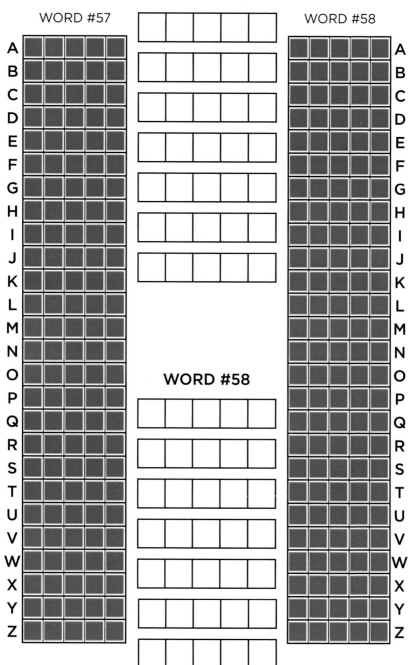

WORD #58

WORD #59

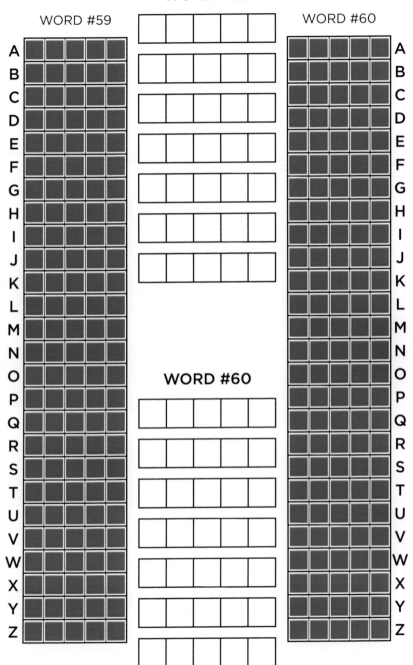

WORD #59

WORD #60

WORD #60

WORD #61

WORD #61

WORD #62

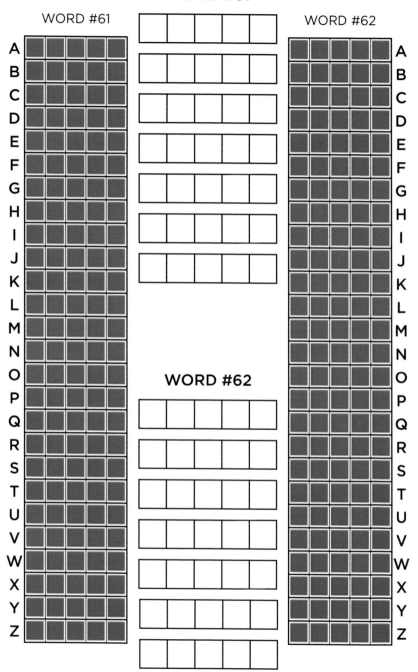

WORD #62

WORD #63

WORD #63

WORD #64

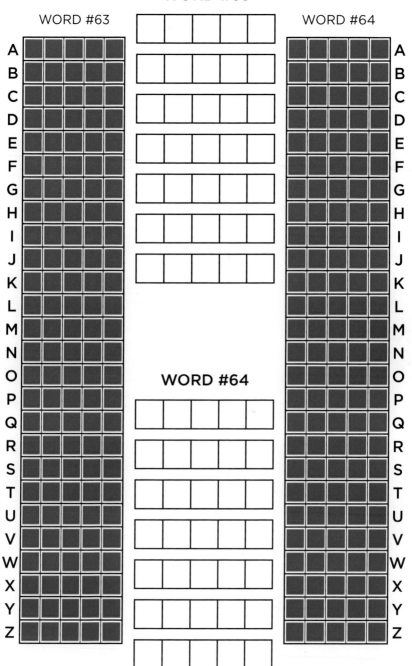

WORD #64

WORD #65

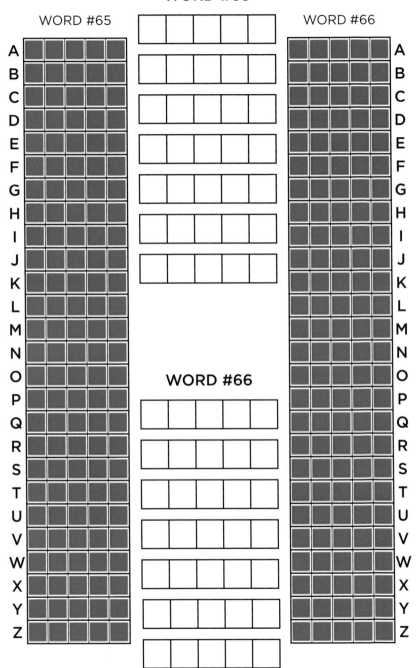

WORD #65

WORD #66

WORD #66

36

WORD #67

WORD #67

A
B
C
D
E
F
G
H
I
J
K
L
M
N
O
P
Q
R
S
T
U
V
W
X
Y
Z

WORD #68

WORD #68

A
B
C
D
E
F
G
H
I
J
K
L
M
N
O
P
Q
R
S
T
U
V
W
X
Y
Z

WORD #69

WORD #69

WORD #70

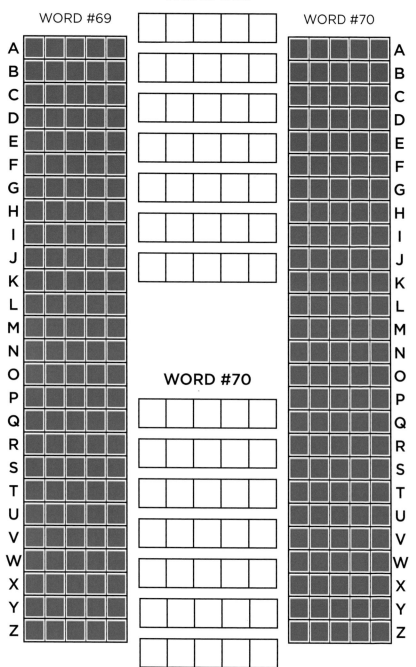

WORD #70

WORD #71

WORD #71

WORD #72

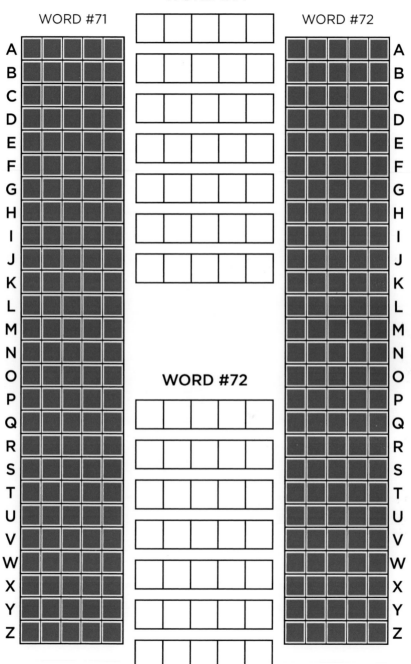

WORD #72

39

WORD #73

WORD #73

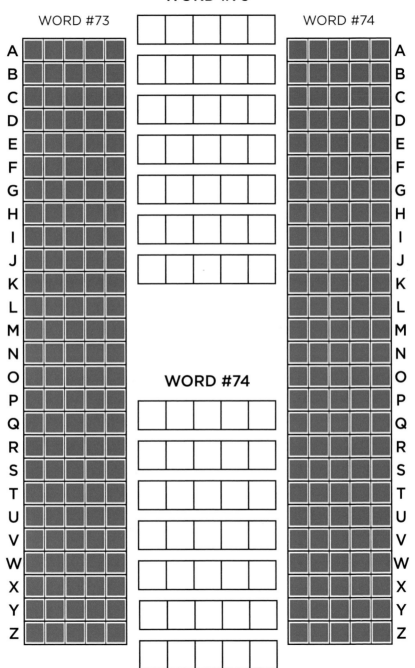

WORD #74

WORD #74

WORD #75

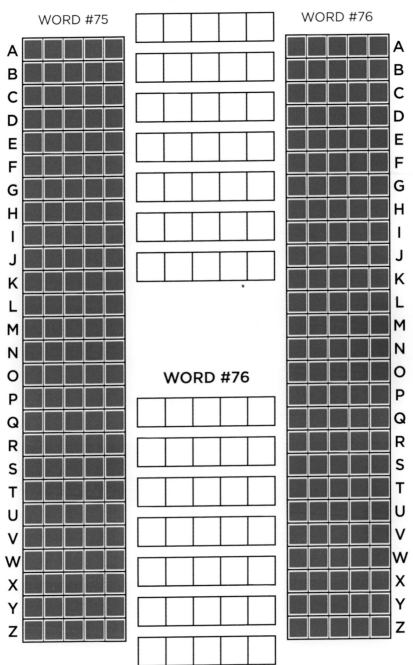

WORD #75

WORD #76

WORD #76

WORD #77

WORD #78

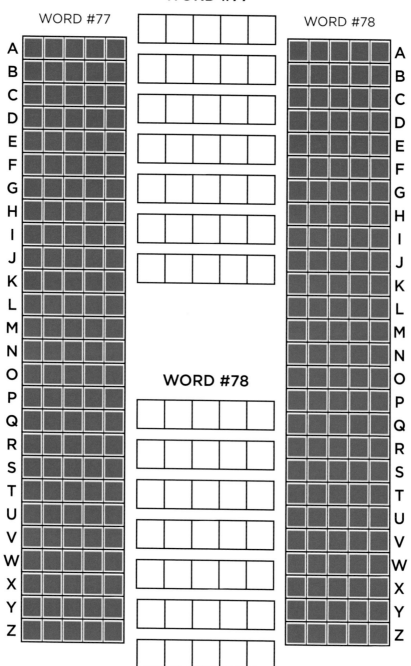

WORD #78

WORD #79

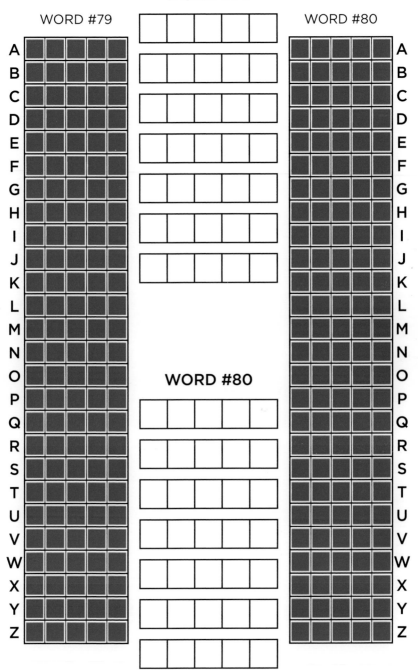

WORD #79

WORD #80

WORD #80

WORD #81

WORD #81

WORD #82

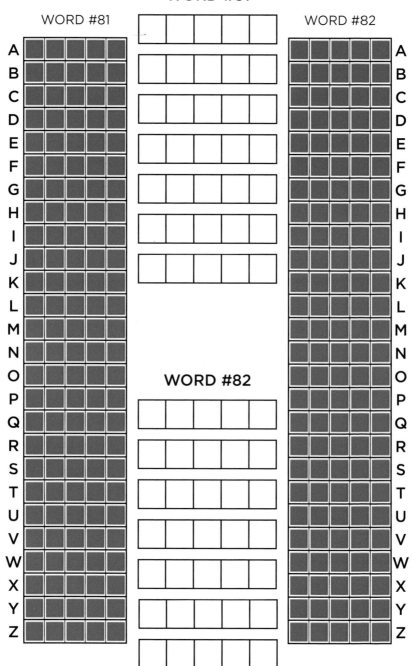

WORD #82

44

WORD #83

WORD #83

WORD #84

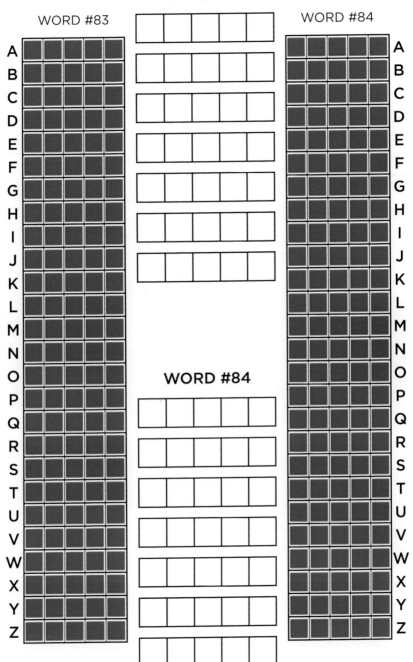

WORD #84

WORD #85

WORD #86

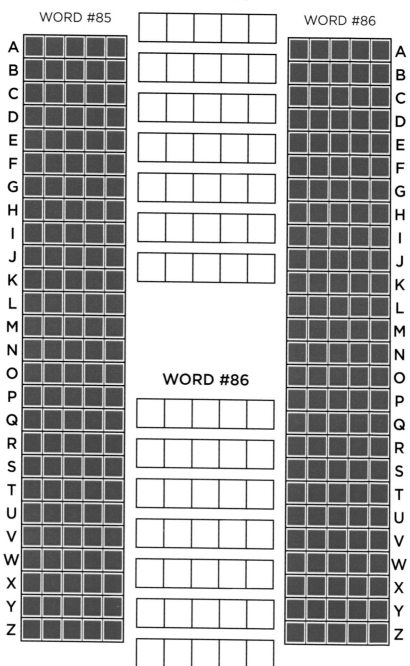

WORD #86

WORD #87

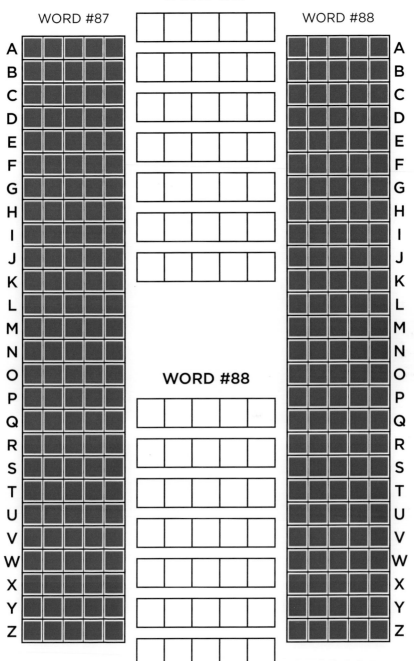

WORD #89

WORD #89

A
B
C
D
E
F
G
H
I
J
K
L
M
N
O
P
Q
R
S
T
U
V
W
X
Y
Z

WORD #90

A
B
C
D
E
F
G
H
I
J
K
L
M
N
O
P
Q
R
S
T
U
V
W
X
Y
Z

WORD #90

WORD #91

WORD #92

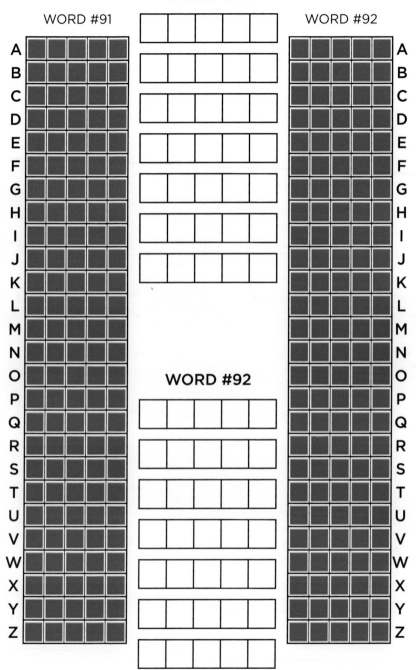

WORD #92

49

WORD #93

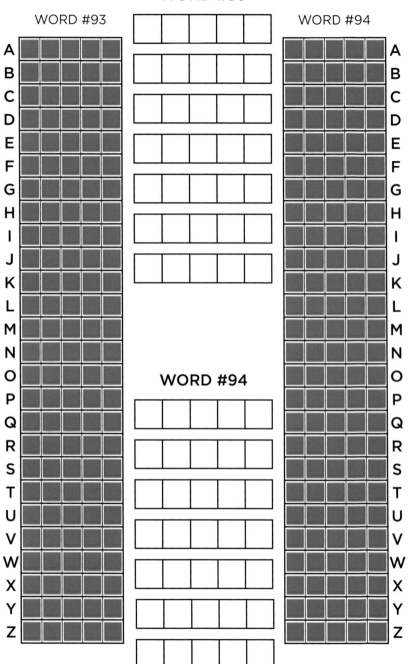

WORD #93

WORD #94

WORD #94

50

WORD #95

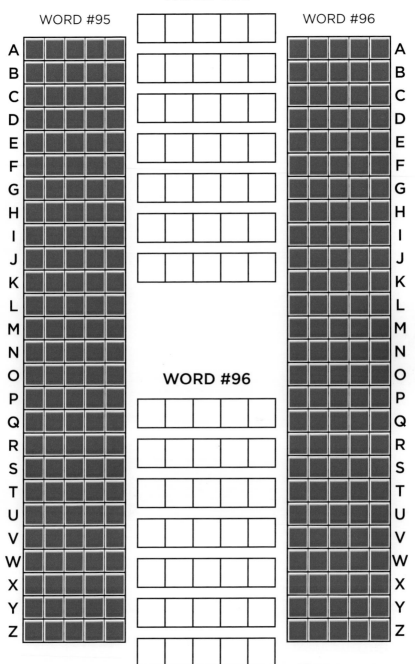

WORD #96

WORD #96

WORD #97

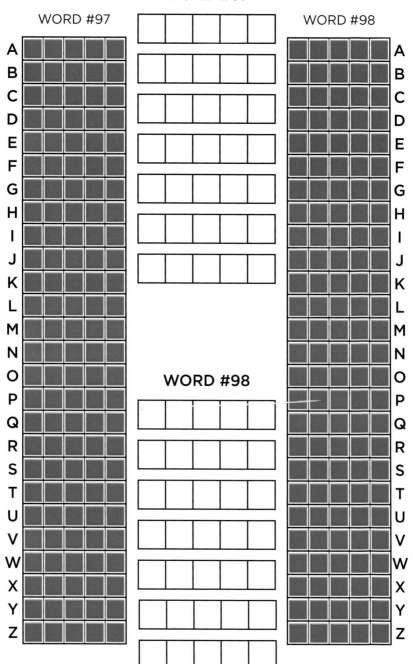

WORD #97

WORD #98

WORD #98

WORD #99

WORD #99

WORD #100

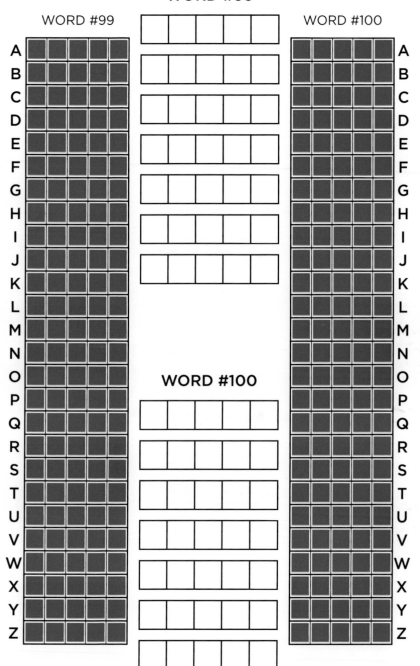

WORD #100

WORD #101

WORD #101

WORD #102

WORD #102

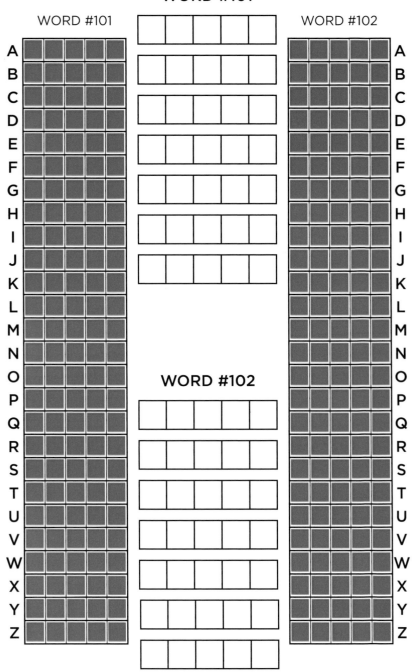

WORD #103

WORD #103

WORD #104

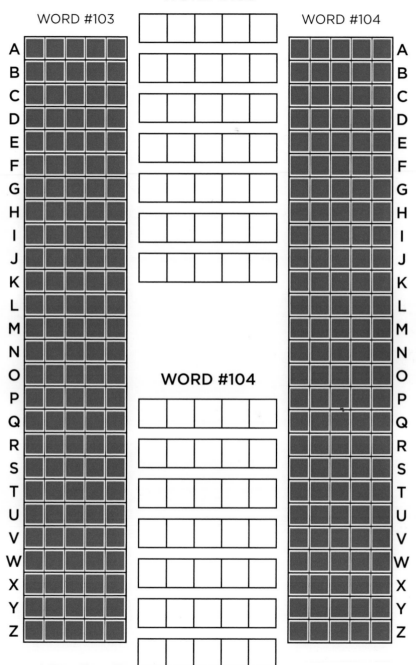

WORD #104

WORD #105

WORD #105

WORD #106

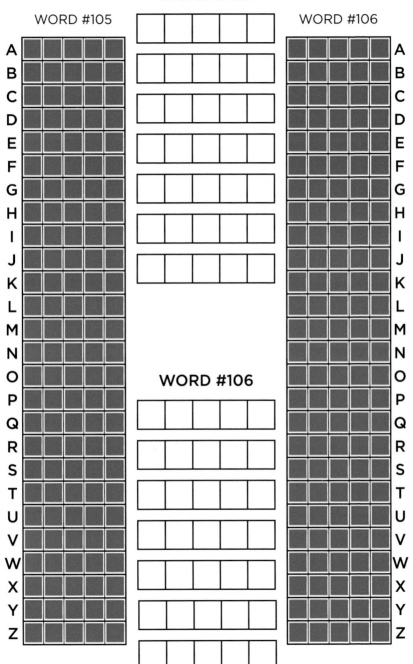

WORD #106

WORD #107

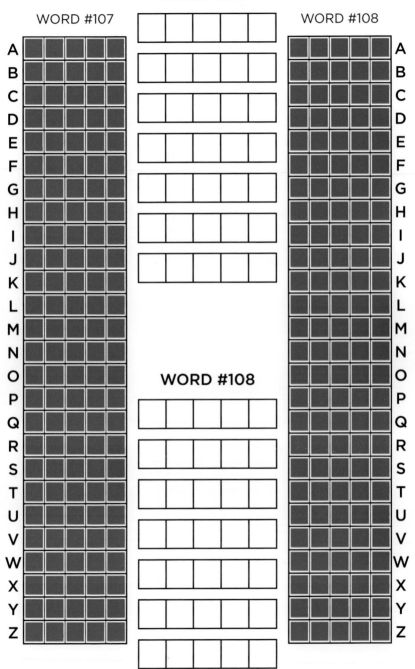

WORD #107

WORD #108

WORD #108

WORD #109

WORD #109

WORD #110

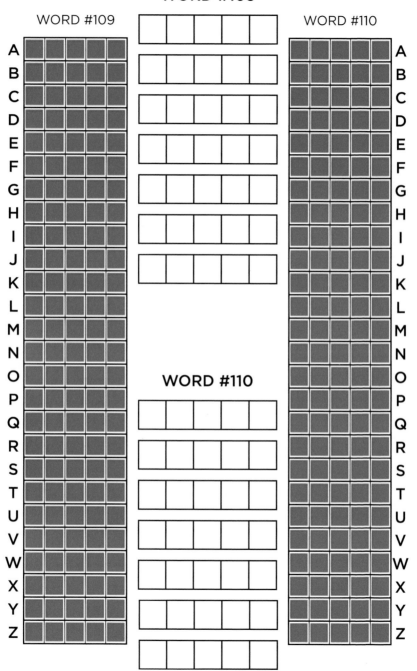

WORD #110

WORD #111

WORD #111

WORD #112

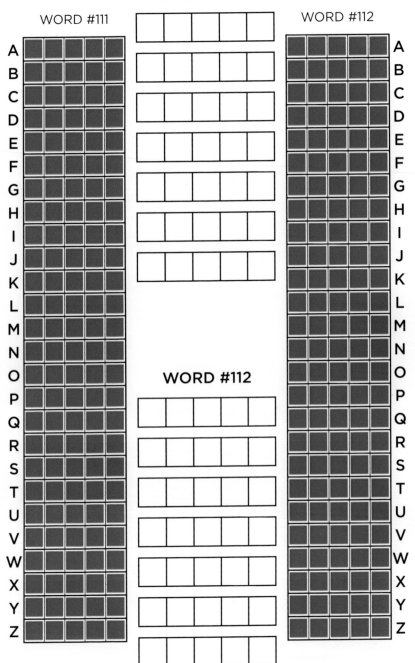

WORD #112

WORD #113

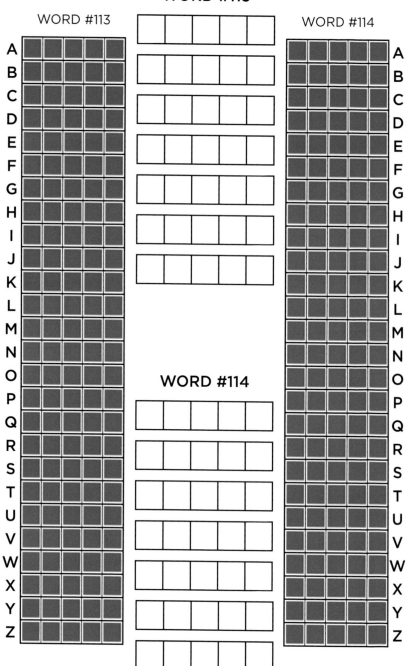

WORD #115

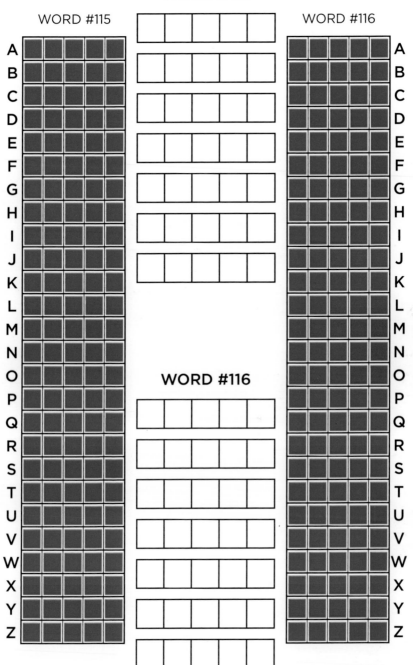

WORD #115

WORD #116

WORD #116

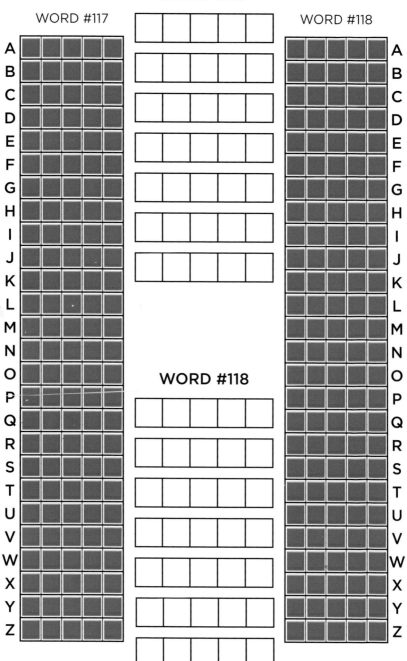

WORD #117

WORD #118

WORD #118

WORD #119

WORD #119

WORD #120

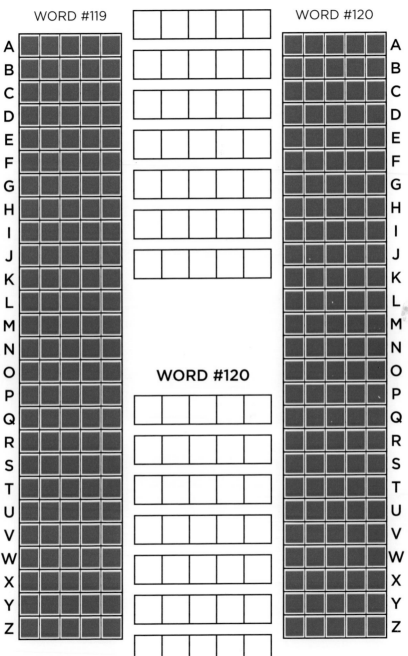

WORD #120

WORD #121

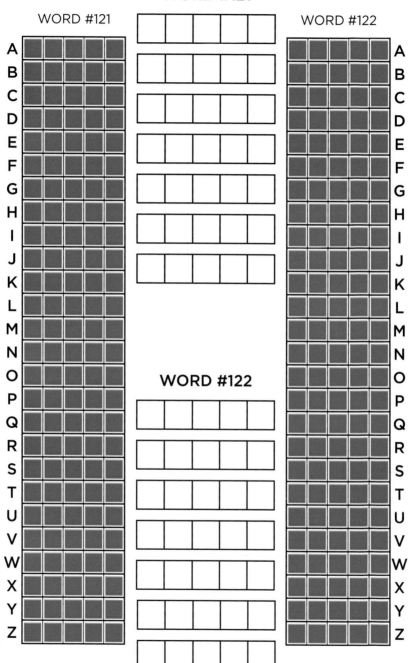

WORD #121

WORD #122

WORD #122

WORD #123

WORD #123

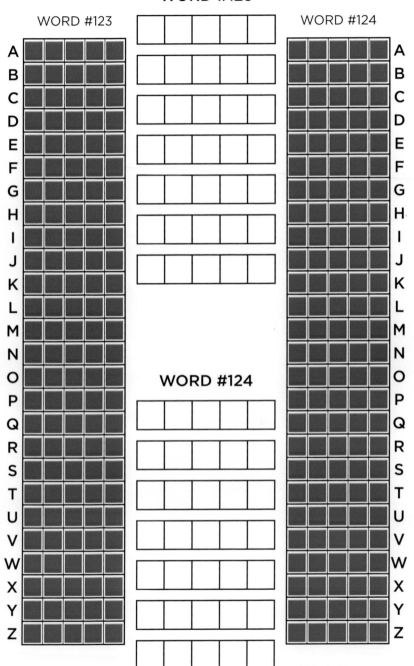

WORD #124

WORD #124

WORD #125

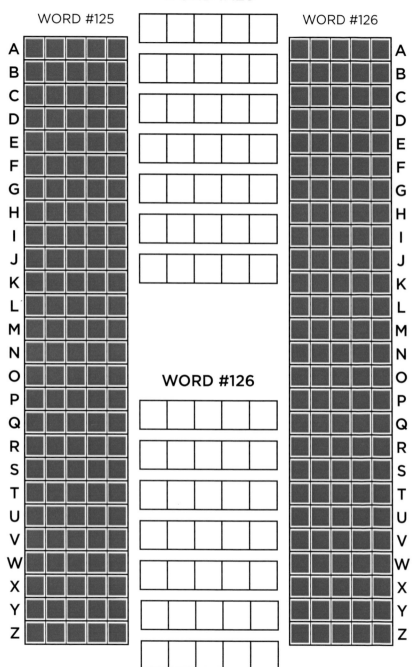

WORD #127

WORD #128

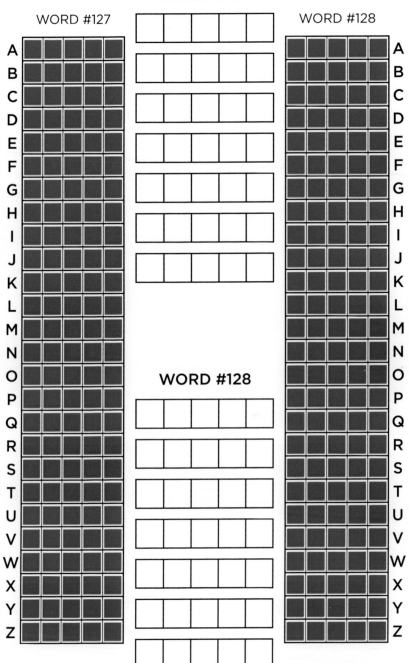

WORD #128

WORD #129

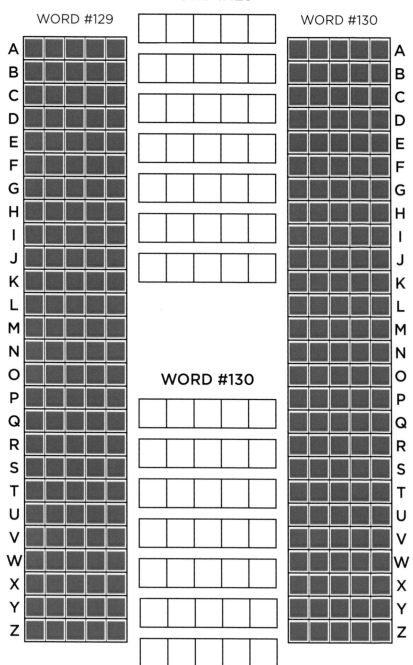

WORD #129

WORD #130

WORD #130

WORD #131

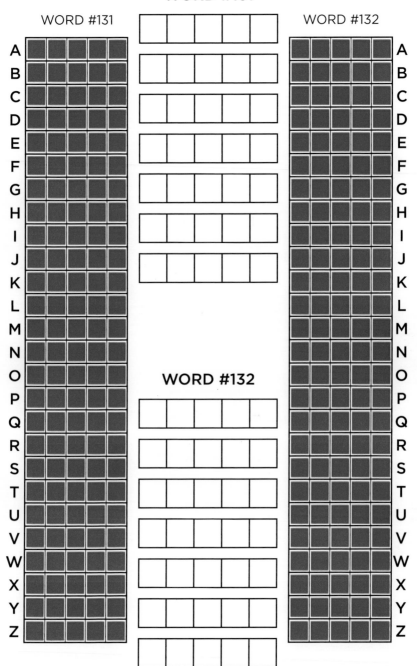

WORD #132

WORD #132

WORD #133

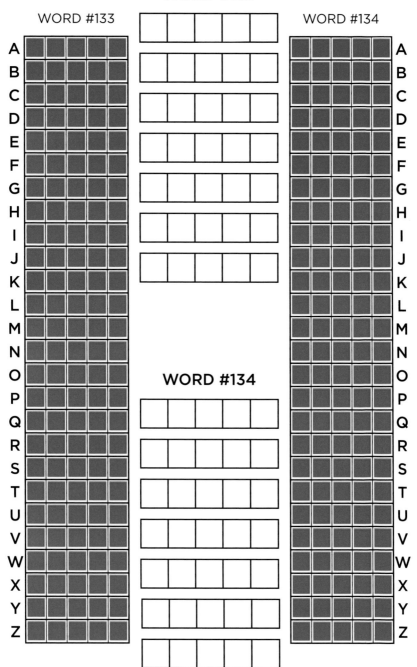

WORD #133

WORD #134

WORD #134

WORD #135

WORD #136

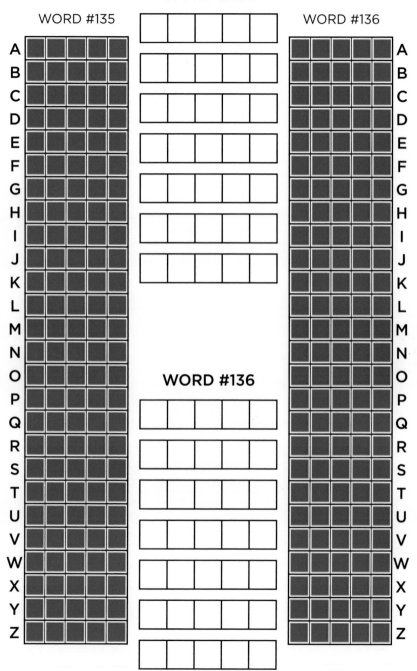

A B C D E F G H I J K L M N O P Q R S T U V W X Y Z

WORD #136

71

WORD #137

WORD #138

A
B
C
D
E
F
G
H
I
J
K
L
M
N
O
P
Q
R
S
T
U
V
W
X
Y
Z

WORD #138

WORD #139

WORD #139

WORD #140

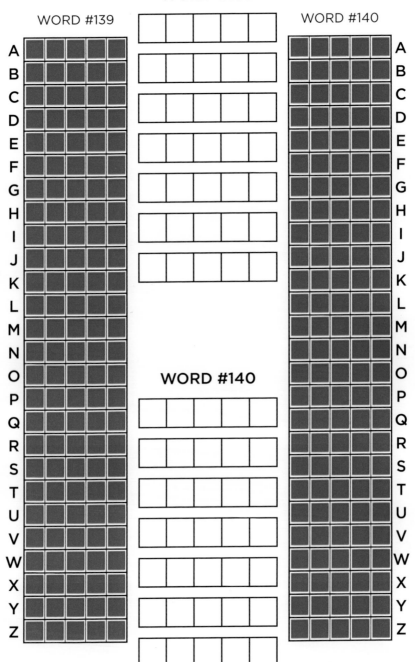

WORD #140

WORD #141

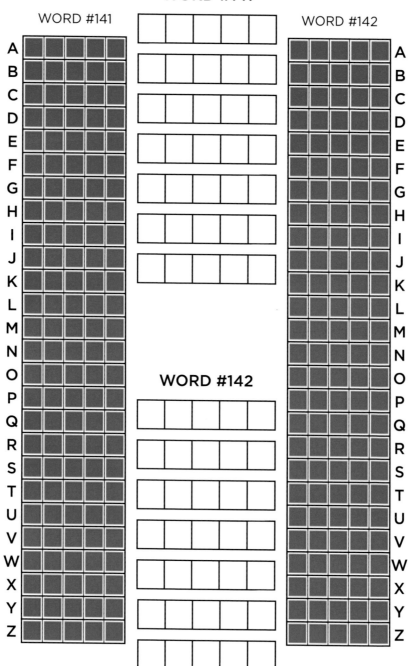

WORD #143

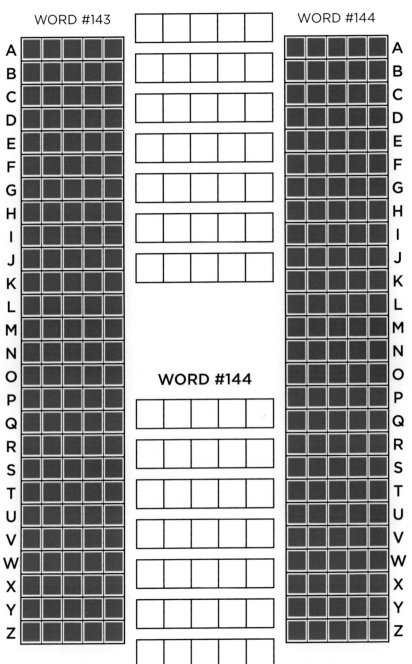

WORD #145

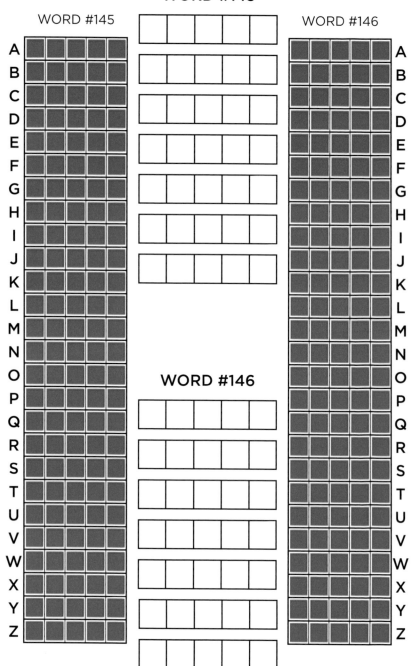

WORD #146

76

WORD #147

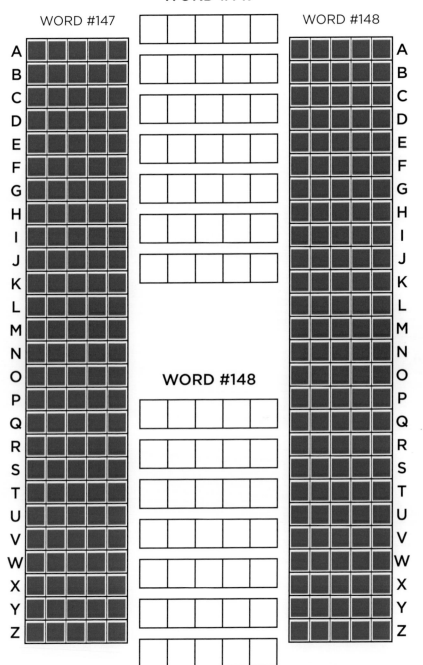

WORD #147

WORD #148

WORD #148

WORD #149

WORD #149

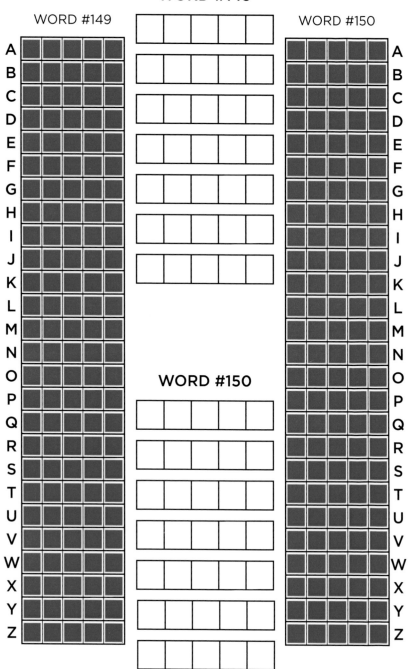

WORD #150

WORD #150

WORD #151

WORD #151

WORD #152

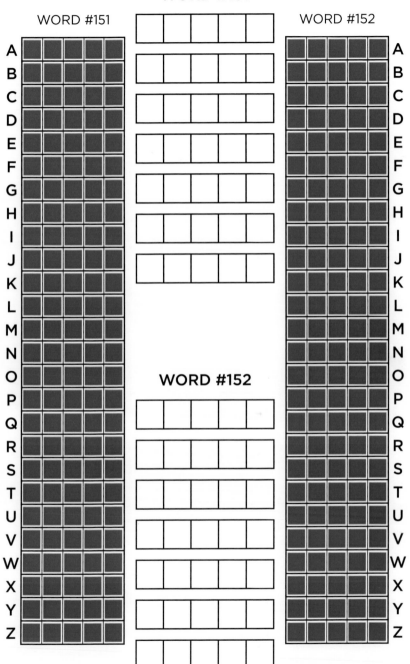

WORD #152

WORD #153

WORD #153

WORD #154

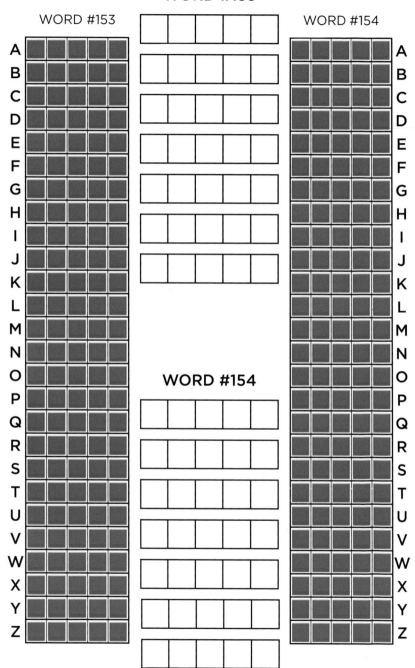

WORD #154

WORD #155

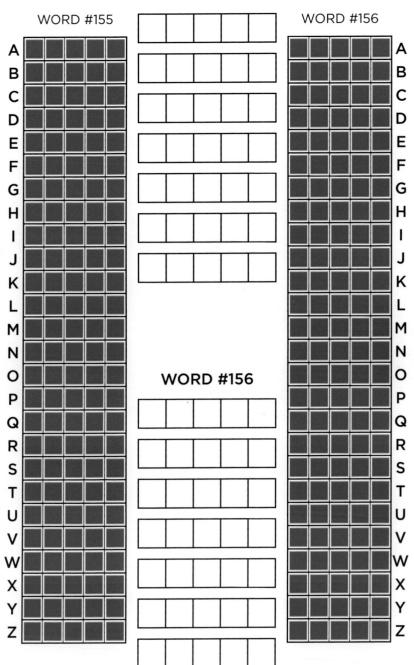

WORD #155

WORD #156

WORD #156

WORD #157

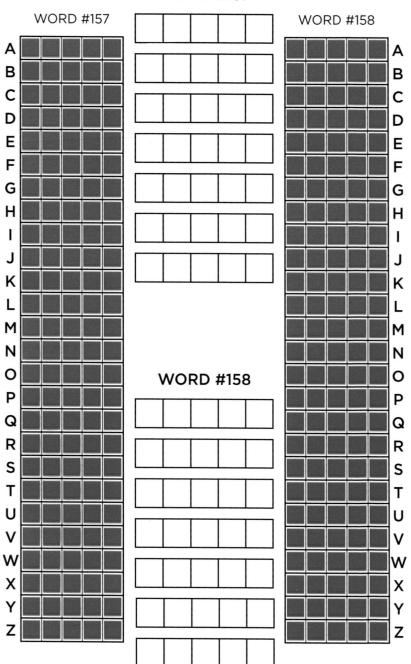

WORD #158

WORD #158

82

WORD #159

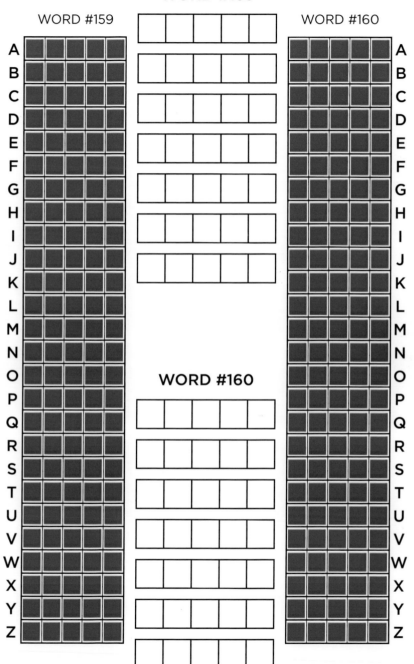

WORD #159

WORD #160

WORD #160

WORD #161

WORD #161

WORD #162

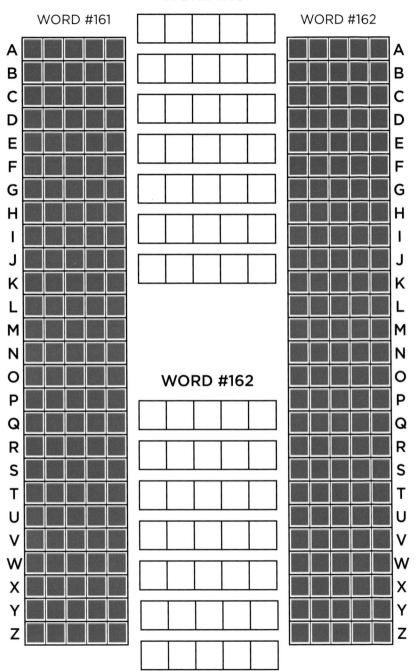

84

WORD #163

WORD #164

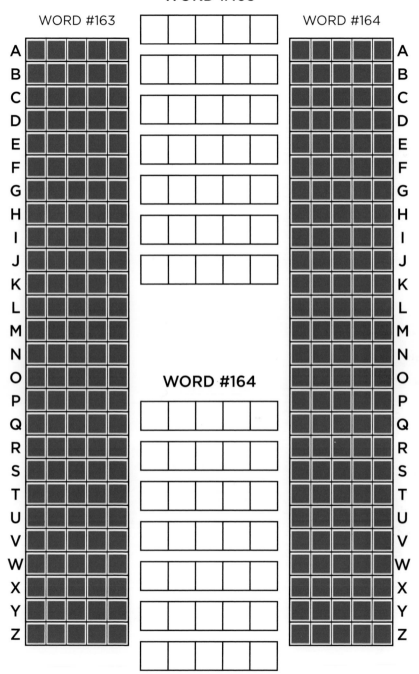

WORD #164

WORD #165

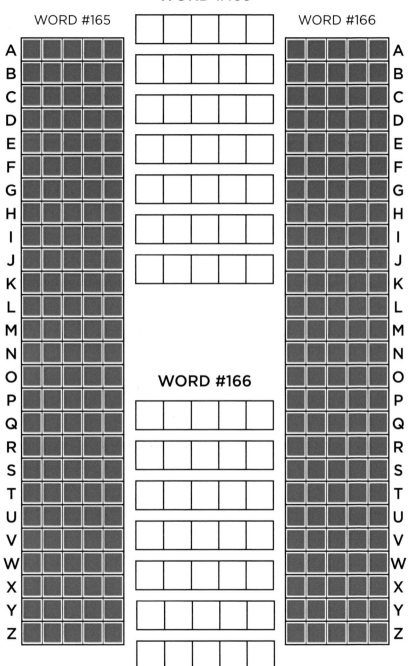

WORD #165

WORD #166

WORD #166

WORD #167

WORD #168

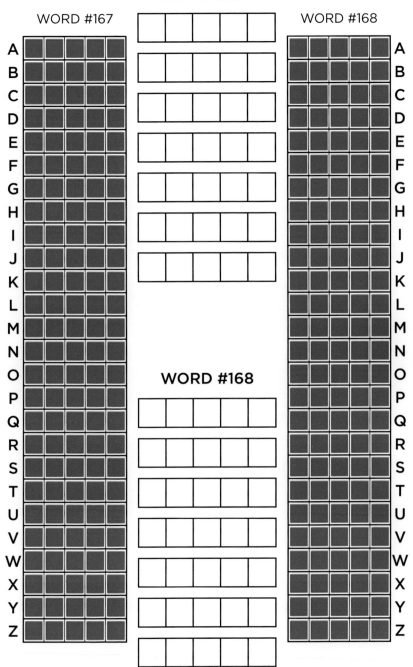

WORD #168

WORD #169

WORD #169

WORD #170

A B C D E F G H I J K L M N O P Q R S T U V W X Y Z

WORD #170

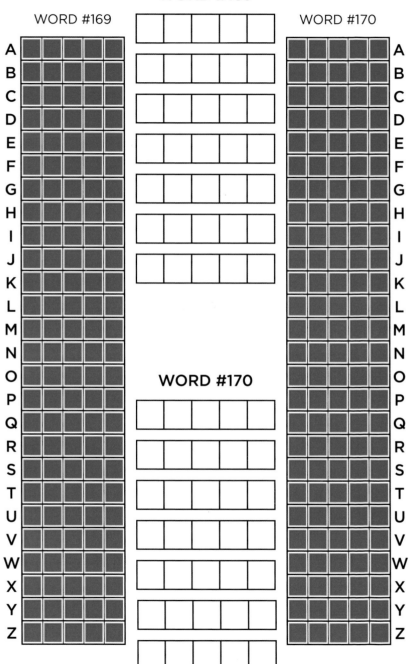

88

WORD #171

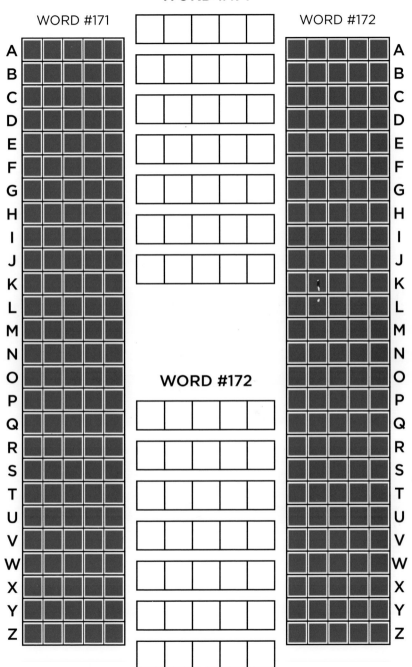

WORD #171

WORD #172

WORD #172

WORD #173

WORD #173

A B C D E F G H I J K L M N O P Q R S T U V W X Y Z

WORD #174

WORD #174

A B C D E F G H I J K L M N O P Q R S T U V W X Y Z

90

WORD #175

WORD #176

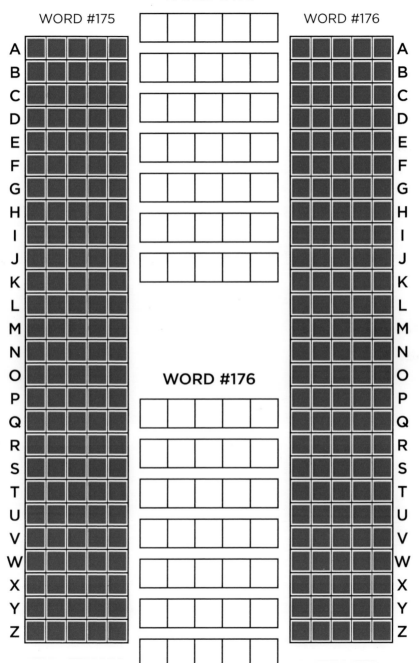

WORD #176

WORD #177

WORD #177

WORD #178

WORD #178

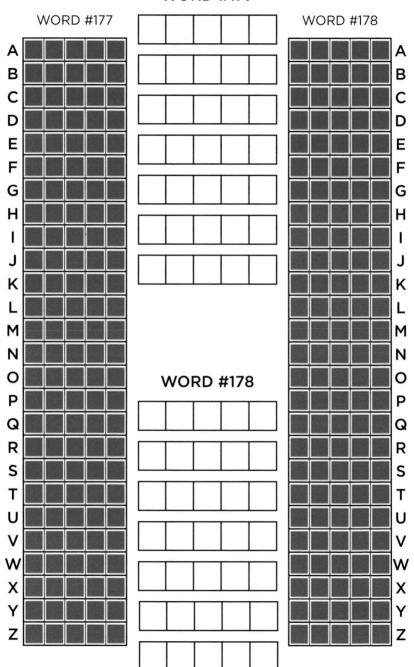

WORD #179

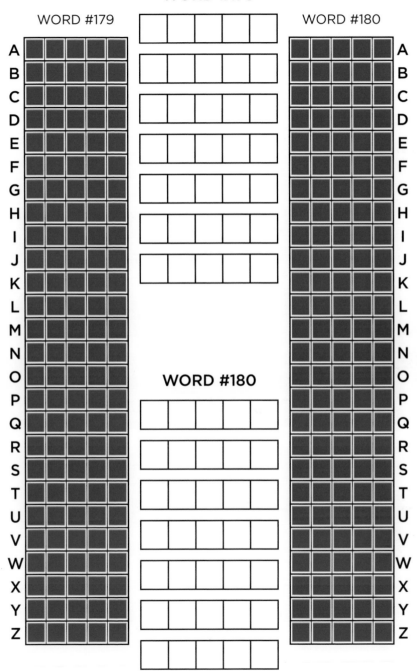

WORD #179

WORD #180

A B C D E F G H I J K L M N O P Q R S T U V W X Y Z

WORD #180

93

WORD #181

WORD #181

WORD #182

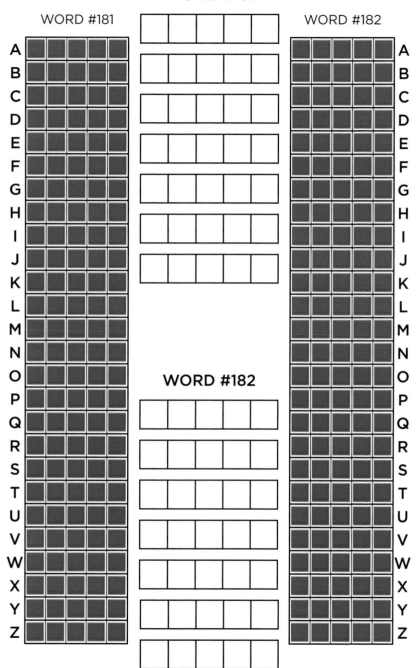

WORD #182

94

WORD #183

WORD #183

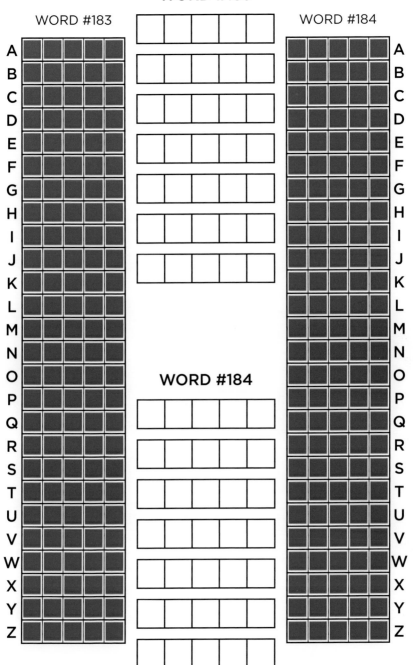

WORD #184

WORD #184

95

WORD #185

WORD #185

WORD #186

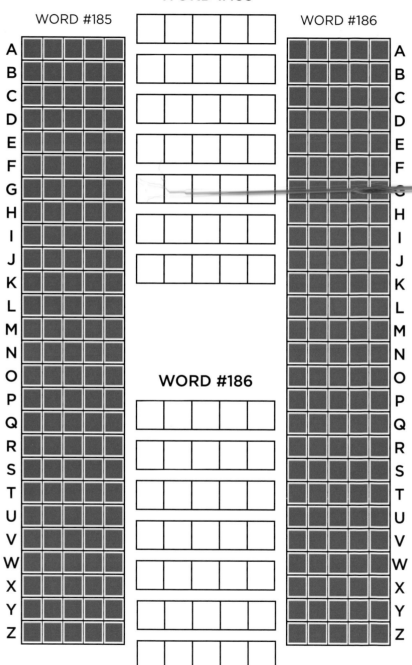

WORD #186

96

WORD #187

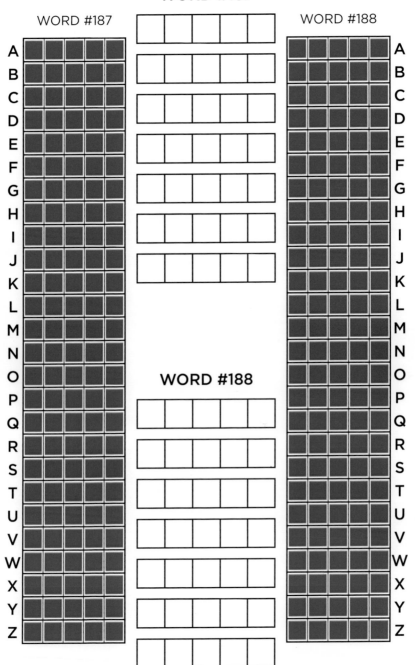

WORD #188

WORD #188

WORD #189

WORD #189

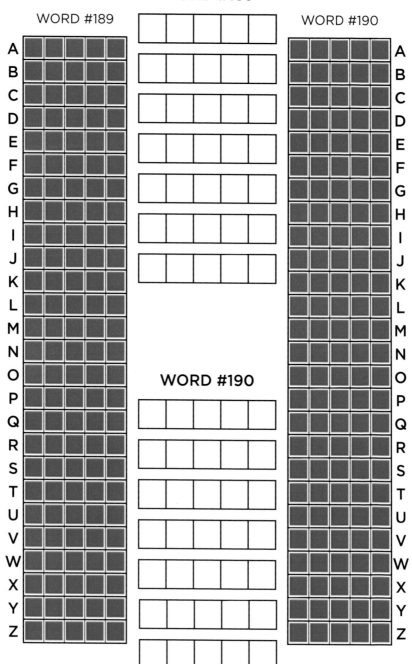

A B C D E F G H I J K L M N O P Q R S T U V W X Y Z

WORD #190

WORD #190

WORD #191

WORD #191

WORD #192

A A
B B
C C
D D
E E
F F
G G
H H
I I
J J
K K
L L
M M
N N
O O
P P
Q Q
R R
S S
T T
U U
V V
W W
X X
Y Y
Z Z

WORD #192

WORD #193

WORD #194

WORD #194

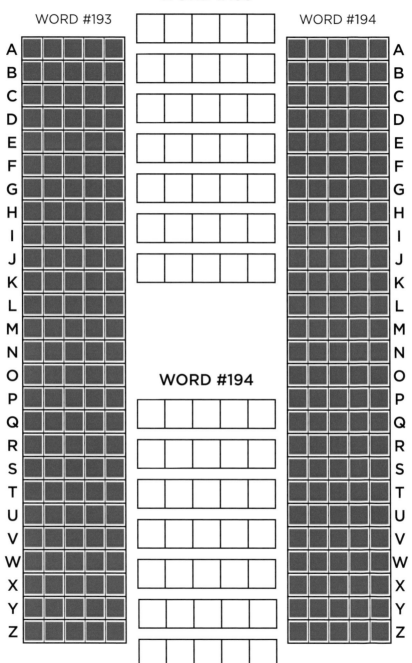

100

WORD #195

WORD #196

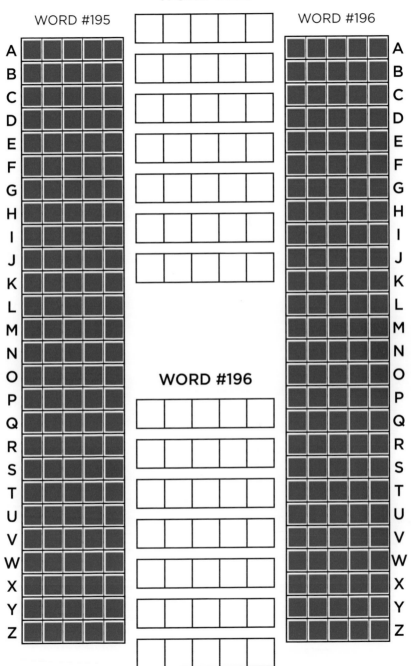

WORD #196

WORD #197

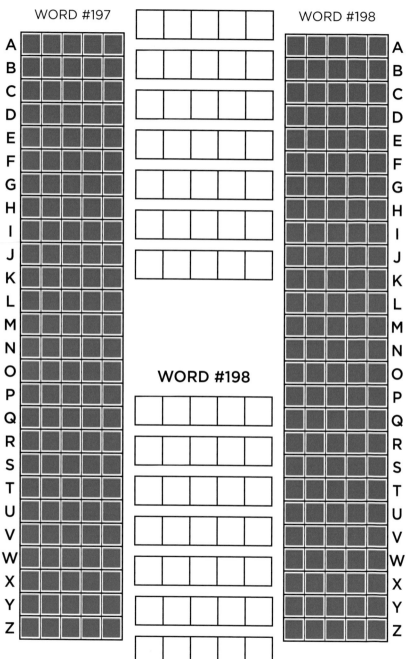

WORD #197

WORD #198

WORD #198

WORD #199

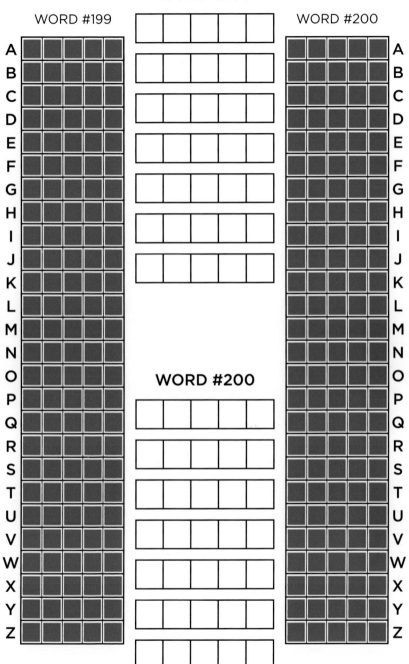

WORD #200

WORD #201

WORD #201

A B C D E F G H I J K L M N O P Q R S T U V W X Y Z

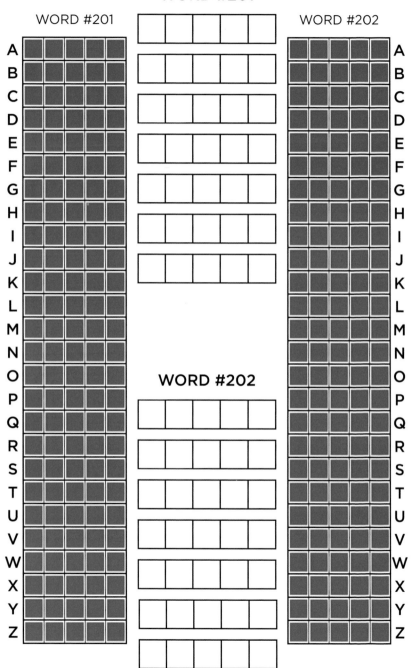

WORD #202

WORD #202

A B C D E F G H I J K L M N O P Q R S T U V W X Y Z

WORD #203

WORD #203

WORD #204

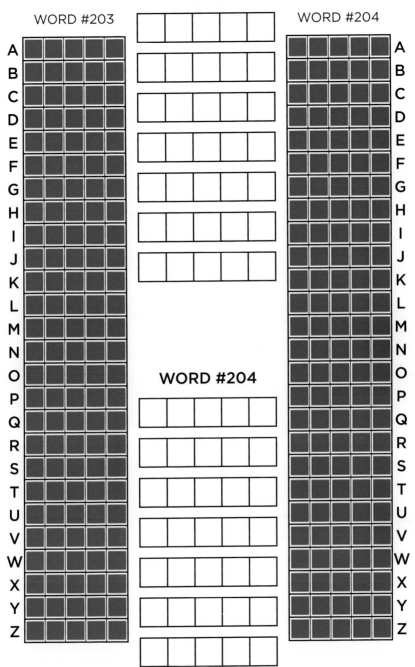

WORD #204

WORD #205

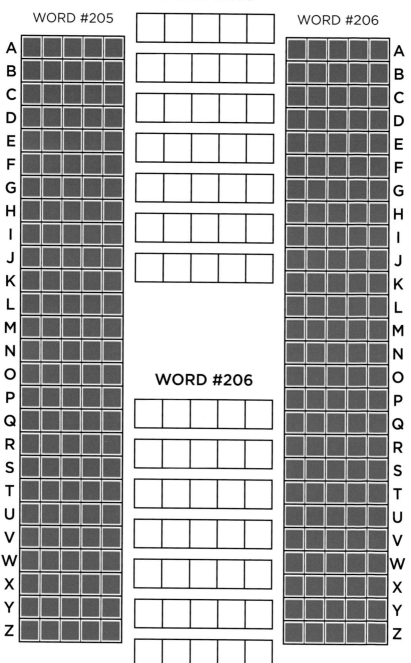

WORD #205

WORD #206

WORD #206

WORD #207

WORD #207

WORD #208

A
B
C
D
E
F
G
H
I
J
K
L
M
N
O
P
Q
R
S
T
U
V
W
X
Y
Z

WORD #208

WORD #209

WORD #209

WORD #210

A B C D E F G H I J K L M N O P Q R S T U V W X Y Z

WORD #210

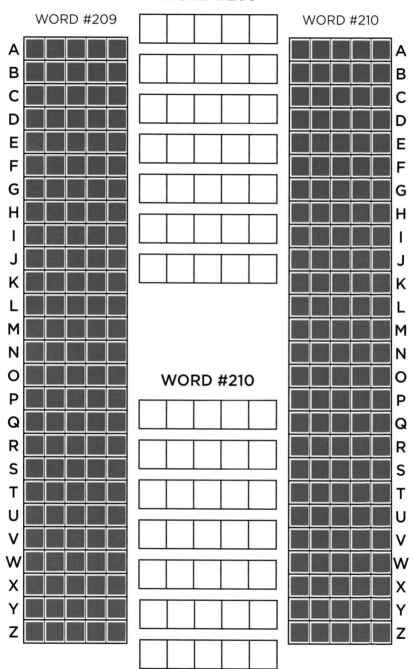

WORD #211

WORD #211

WORD #212

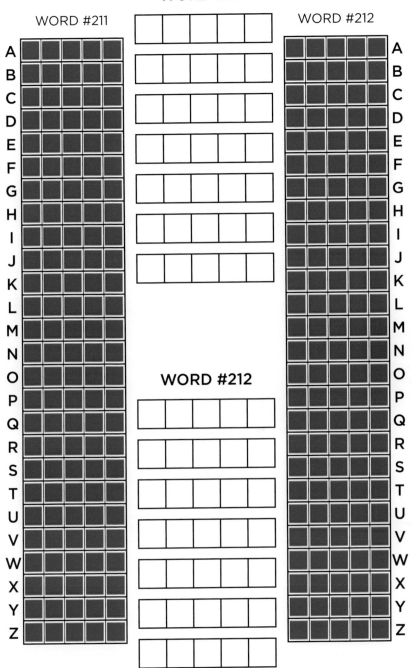

WORD #212

WORD #213

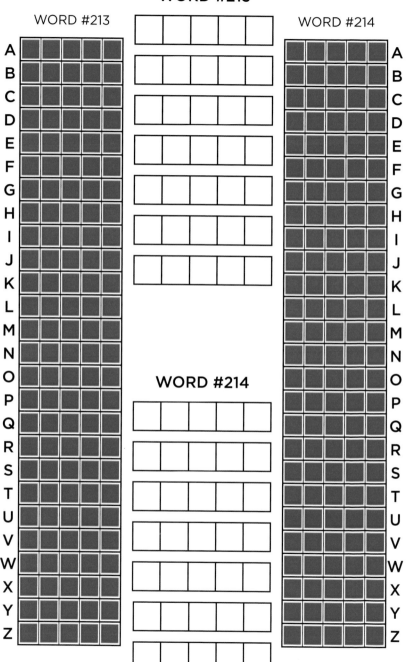

WORD #214

WORD #214

WORD #215

WORD #215

WORD #216

WORD #216

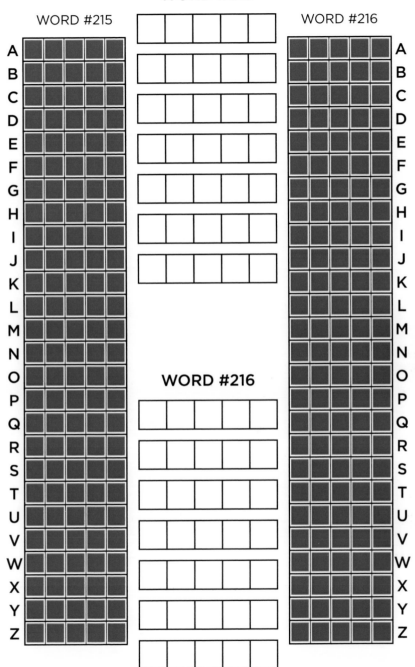

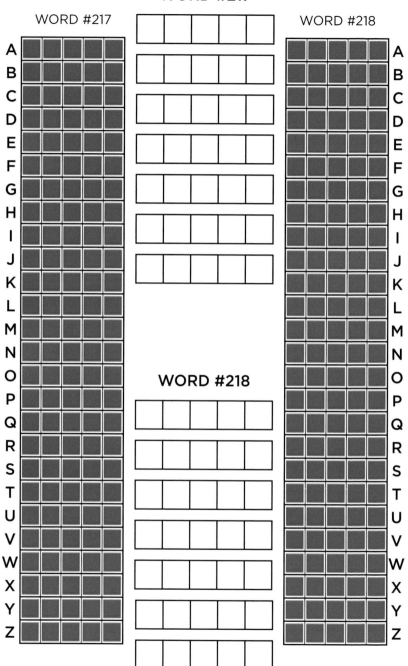

WORD #217

WORD #218

WORD #218

WORD #219

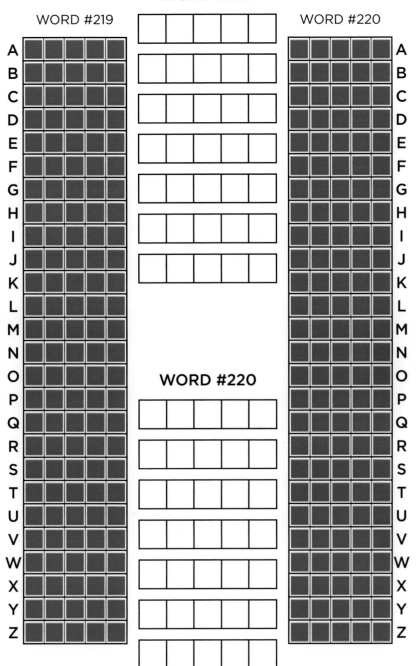

WORD #219

WORD #220

WORD #220

WORD #221

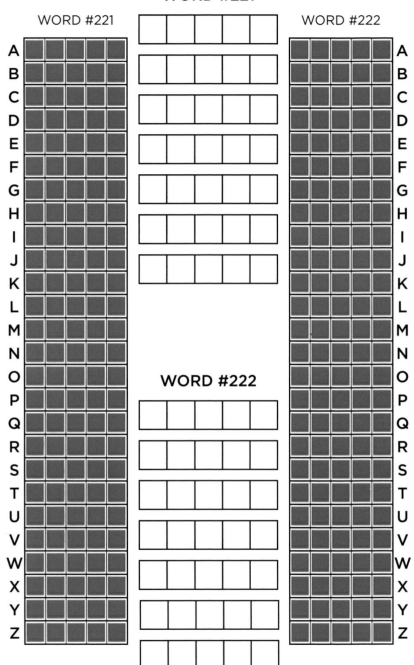

WORD #222

WORD #223

WORD #223

WORD #224

A
B
C
D
E
F
G
H
I
J
K
L
M
N
O
P
Q
R
S
T
U
V
W
X
Y
Z

WORD #224

WORD #225

WORD #225

WORD #226

A B C D E F G H I J K L M N O P Q R S T U V W X Y Z

WORD #227

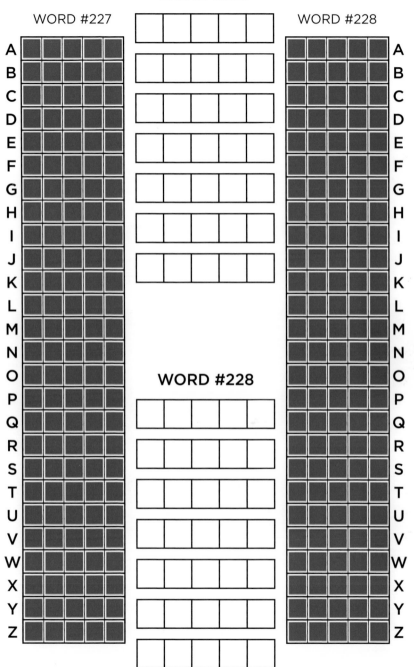

WORD #227

WORD #228

WORD #228

WORD #229

WORD #229

WORD #230

A
B
C
D
E
F
G
H
I
J
K
L
M
N
O
P
Q
R
S
T
U
V
W
X
Y
Z

WORD #230

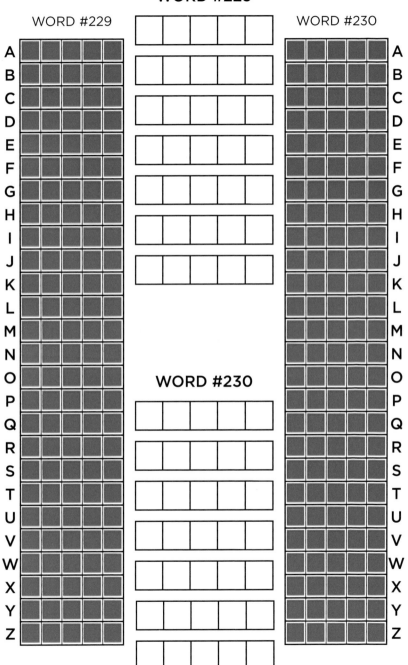

WORD #231

WORD #231

WORD #232

A
B
C
D
E
F
G
H
I
J
K
L
M
N
O
P
Q
R
S
T
U
V
W
X
Y
Z

WORD #232

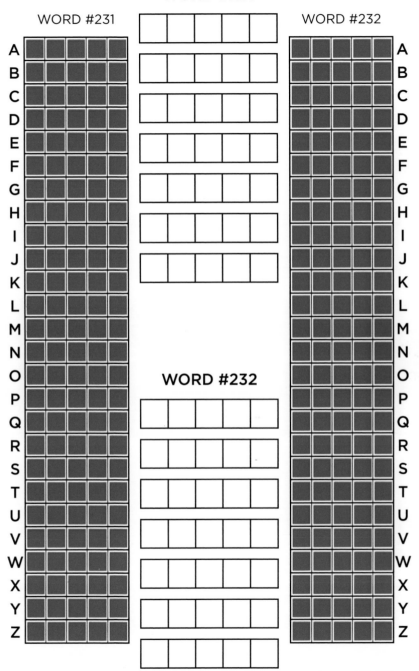

WORD #233

WORD #234

WORD #234

120

WORD #235

WORD #236

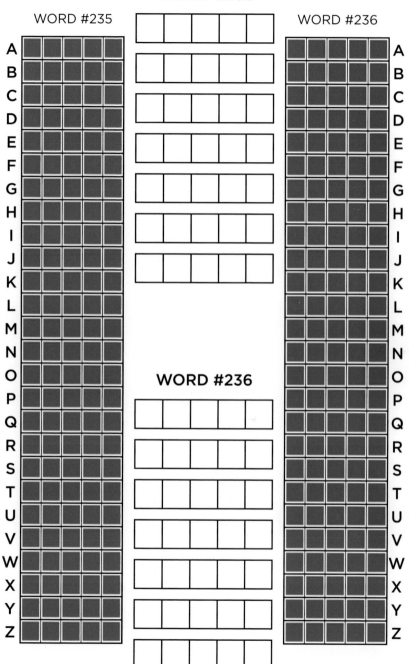

WORD #236

WORD #237

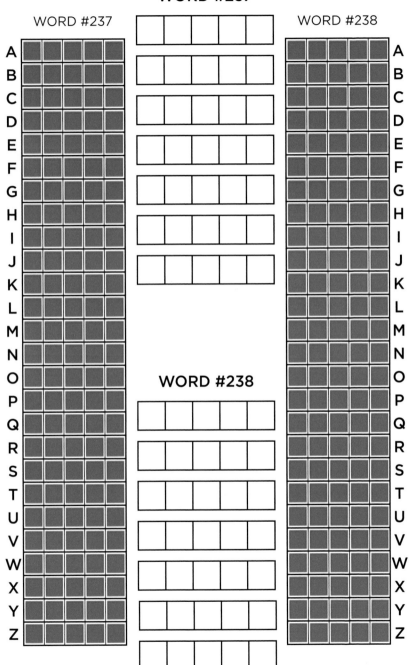

WORD #237

WORD #238

WORD #238

A B C D E F G H I J K L M N O P Q R S T U V W X Y Z

WORD #239

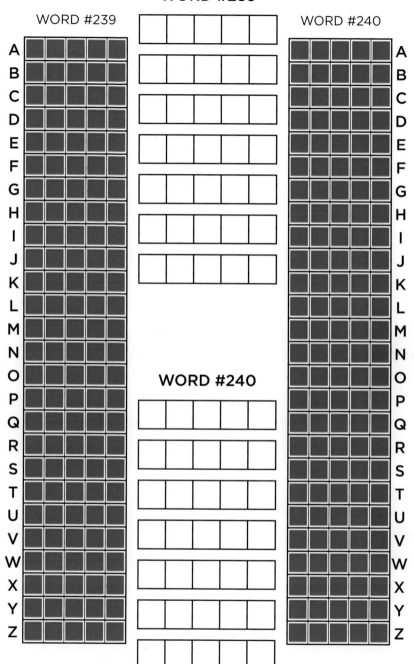

WORD #240

WORD #240

WORD #241

WORD #241

WORD #242

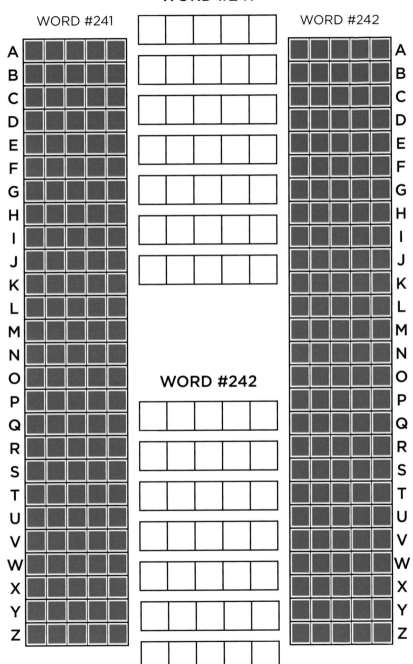

124

WORD #243

WORD #243

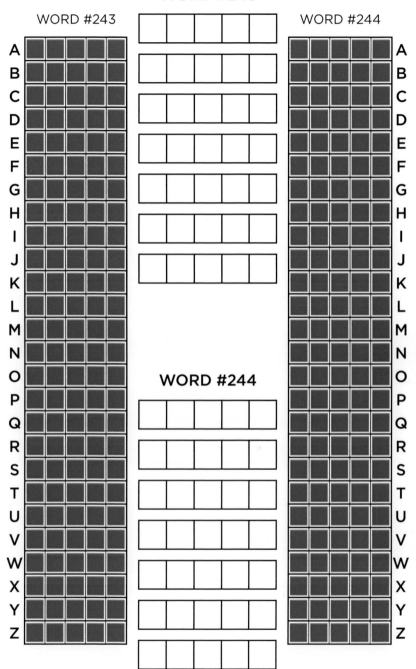

WORD #244

WORD #244

WORD #245

WORD #246

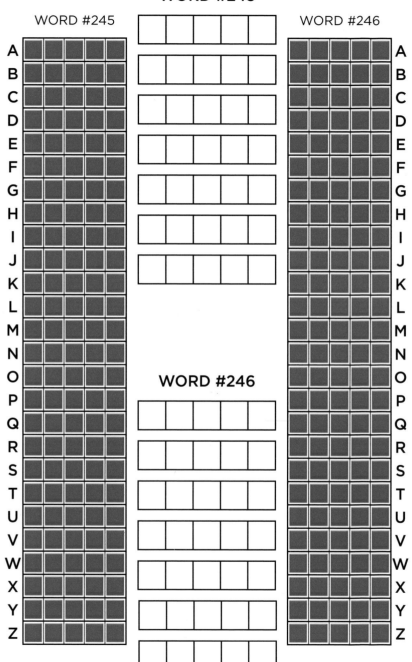

WORD #246

126